PUBLIC SCHOOLS OF WASHINGTON.

ADDRESS

OF

HON. JOSEPH R. CHANDLER,

OF PENNSYLVANIA,

AT THE

PUBLIC SCHOOL CELEBRATION,

AUGUST 1, 1850.

WASHINGTON:
PRINTED BY JOHN T. TOWERS.
1850.

PUBLIC SCHOOLS OF WASHINGTON.

ADDRESS

OF

HON. JOSEPH R. CHANDLER,

OF PENNSYLVANIA,

AT THE

PUBLIC SCHOOL CELEBRATION,

AUGUST 1, 1850.

WASHINGTON:
PRINTED BY JOHN T. TOWERS.
1850.

WASHINGTON, (D. C.) AUGUST 2, 1850.

DEAR SIR: We have been authorized by the Trustees of the Public Schools of the City of Washington to tender to you their thanks for the very appropriate and excellent Address with which you favored them on the 1st instant, and respectfully request a copy of it for publication.

Very respectfully, yours,

R. FARNHAM,
V. HARBAUGH,
J. M. ROBERTS,
P. M. PEARSON,
G. J. ABBOT,
CHAS. A. DAVIS,
Committee of Arrangements.

Hon. JOSEPH R. CHANDLER.

HOUSE OF REPRESENTATIVES,
WASHINGTON, AUGUST 5, 1850.

GENTLEMEN: The hastily prepared Address made to the Scholars, Teachers, and Trustees of the Public Schools of Washington, is at your service, and a copy thereof is herewith sent.

I am, very truly, your obedient servant,

JOS. R. CHANDLER.

R. FARNHAM, V. HARBAUGH, J. M. ROBERTS, P. M. PEARSON, G. J. ABBOT, CHAS. A. DAVIS, Esquires, *Committee of Arrangements.*

PREFACE.

The examination of the Public Schools of Washington city, during the month of July, 1850, was probably more thorough than at any former period of their existence; and public attention was attracted to them in a manner not previously known. They had evidently prospered during the preceding year; the teachers and pupils had been inspired with a spirit of emulation, and the expectations of the public had been aroused. Citizens of Washington, previously indifferent to the subject, appeared suddenly impressed with the conviction that these schools might be institutions of public utility, and therefore worthy of their fostering care.

This was readily discerned by the Board of Trustees, who hence resolved that the cause of popular education in Washington should be advanced by means of this happy combination of favoring circumstances; and they accordingly determined upon a public display of the schools, that they might thus confirm the favorable impressions already made upon the popular mind, and arrest the attention of the many thousands who yet remained uninformed in relation to this important matter.

In pursuance of this resolve, the schools, to the number of nearly two thousand pupils, with their teachers, were paraded in uniform, and with music, on Thursday, the first day of August. The exhibition was one of unsurpassed beauty, and attracted the notice of the entire community. Thousands upon thousands of people thronged the streets through which the procession was to pass, and accompanied it to the beautiful grounds east of the Capitol. Here a platform had been erected, and while the schools were marshalled into lines in front of it, and the spectators occupied the wide area beyond, the Trustees of the Schools, headed by the Mayor and Councils of the city, ascended, conducting to their assigned places the distinguished personages who were to participate in the ceremonies of the day. Amongst these was Millard Fillmore, President of the United States, who had with characteristic kindness and courtesy consented to distribute the premiums awarded to industry and merit.

The scene was one of great moral beauty. The members of the City Councils, from whom alone aid had ever been invoked, and whose annual appropriations had so often encountered the most formidable opposition, were now permitted to witness the strongest indications of improvement in the popular sentiment. The Chief Executive Officer of the Nation, upon whom devolve responsibilities of the most momentous importance, had deemed the occasion one not only meriting the influence of his name and presence, but his sincere solicitude.

The array of the schools was beautifully imposing. Their banners, numerous and richly ornamented, were placed around the platform, which they elegantly adorned. The boys were gaily decked with the regalia of their respective districts, generally in uniform; the girls were in white, and wore flowers as their appropriate adornments, in many instances in wreaths upon their heads; while the Teachers stood in the midst of their scholars to control and protect them.

This scene, though every voice were mute, was well adapted to win the admiration of each beholder, and cause him to proclaim the truth that the most solemn duty of our lives is to cherish and instruct the youth of our country, to educate for usefulness and honor, and save from ignorance and woe.

The stillness was broken by the voice of the Rev. Mr. GURLEY, who eloquently invoked of the Throne of Grace a blessing upon the united desires of all there assembled. The Orator selected for the occasion was then introduced by W. LENOX, Esq., Mayor of Washington, and in an earnest and impressive manner delivered the Address we would here commend to the perusal of all who can respond to the sentiments of philanthropy, embodied in the language of beauty and of eloquence. The speaker appeared but to give definiteness and utterance to the vague impulses preconceived by the thousands who heard him; and the convictions he brought to their minds will live as a monument of his devotion to the welfare of our youth.

The kind and benignant words addressed by the President to each pupil as he presented the awarded medals, fell gratefully upon the heart; and they will be remembered and repeated as the words of high encouragement through many coming years. Thus, in the fields of philanthropy and benevolence a little germ will often produce the richest and most abundant fruits of beneficence.

The cause of popular education in the District of Columbia has now, it is hoped, received the seal and signet of the public approval. In the past, the Public Schools of Washington have known little else than the darkness of adversity. The future presents hopes of brighter fortunes. With such aid as has been given to the Public Schools of several of the States of this Union, ours will no doubt become models for the people of many portions of the Republic. Unaided in the future as in the past, save by the slender means of our own citizens, they will still live to bless the young, and to reflect honor upon the friends who sustained them in the dark struggles of their early existence.

ADDRESS.

One of the most beautiful sights in a tropical climate is, I am told, the exhibition of trees, where at once is presented every form, from the undeveloped bud to the ripened fruit; where the eye rests upon the delicate blossom whose odors pour sweets upon the air, and at the same time the luscious fruits tempts the palate to a constant indulgence. To the philanthropist the present scene, partaking of the same variety, must afford a yet higher gratification; for here the flower gives forth its sweetness, here the immature fruit swells into rivalry with its ripened antecedent, and here, dropping from the branches by which it has been sustained, and which it has ornamented, the decaying product bids a welcome to its successor and departs. All ages and all conditions come up to the annual festival; each presents his appropriate form; each is sustained by its proper feelings, hopes, or remembrances.

I am invited hither, not to reward the mature or the aged for their sacrifices, and the weariness consequent upon their attendance, but to offer a few words to these younger ones who make the display, and whose special holiday it is. To them belongs the occasion, for their pleasure it was ordained. Let us hope, while it is certainly to the honor of their seniors, that it will be for their own benefit.

My young friends, I offer to you my hearty congratulations upon the evidences of improvement in knowledge, and upon the real pleasure which the display of this evening presents, and I invite you to turn back your thoughts for one year, that you may more readily comprehend the benefits which have been prepared for you by the directors of the schools, and which you have secured to yourselves by your own application and the assistance of your beloved teachers. I use the term "beloved" with regard to your teachers without knowing one of them, because I understand that you have made great improvement; and let me assure you that no considerable attainments are ever made by the scholar without a love for the instructor. That affection is the first great means, or it is an early consequence and then a principal agent in the acquisition of knowledge.

Look back, my young friends, and see what has been your improvement for one year: and then remember that all such improvement is made for life; it is secured to you as long as you shall live, and it is the only property that you have secured. You have it now, and you have it with the consequent interest and advantages forever. Hundreds who, twelve months since, were comfortable in all their circumstances, are now in the depths of poverty; hundreds who, within that time, have attained competency may in a few months be left destitute; but that wealth of the mind—that commencement of intellectual riches which results from your year's studies, can know no diminution: it is self-accumulative, and increases through all time by its own attraction.

I had not the pleasure of attending the annual examination by which your new attainments in school knowledge were tested by the teachers and exhibited to the world, but I hear that you acquitted yourselves with great credit, and did honor to those entrusted with your education. It could scarcely be otherwise; the system of the schools is good. Your teachers are skilful and faithful: of course you have applied yourselves, and you have rapidly advanced in all the branches of school knowledge which you have been called to study. Knowledge of reading, penmanship, arithmetic, history, grammar, geography, the foundation and material of that knowledge without which man's and woman's estate towards which you tend, and for which you are impatient, would lack that honor and respectability which renders age desirable. These you have, of course, begun to acquire, and you have also begun to see their advantages. It is perhaps enough to say, whatever may have been the circumstances of other times, that in the present age and the age of which you are to form an important part, no man or woman can be useful—can claim even respectability—if destitute of that knowledge which you are beginning to acquire. Such a knowledge, such attainments are so much the necessaries of life, their importance are so obvious, you, indeed, begin now to see the advantages so plainly, that I will not further recommend them to you, nor further recommend you to pursue them.

There are other attainments which belong to your years to which I desire to call your attention. You notice that all the studies to which I have referred may be pursued with much success by children who are not distinguished by any excellence of character. As all the knowledge which you have, and which you are trying to have, may be attained in an eminent degree by very bad persons, though I agree that the very habit of obedience and attention and order necessary to the successful studies of a school, tends toward a proper regulation of the mind, and the establishment of correct moral habits.

But all the studies to which I have referred have reference to the head—they make what is denominated the cultivation of the intellect. You have hearts as well as heads, my young friends, and you have affections as well as intellect. Let me say to you, you must learn to improve the heart. You must endeavor to cultivate the affections, and in this great branch of human study, young as you are, you must in a great measure be your own teachers.

These schools of which you form a part are called public schools, because they are sustained by the public and for the public. They are called common schools because the education acquired in them is to be common to all. Each one of you is stimulated to study hard, to apply closely—not that any one of you may exceed the other—not that it is desired that one boy or girl should have superior knowledge. Each one is urged that each and every one may, by application, attain all that any other acquires.

You see then that the object is to make you all learned; to place you all on the same platform of knowledge, just as you all occupy the same political platform of equality. But of what use would this equality be? What advantage to you or others would accrue from your standing side by side, if you did not regard each other kindly? Of what benefit would your attainments in knowledge be, if you did not love one another? If you have grown up in hate, then the greater the inequality, the wider the difference between you, the better for you and for all: if you have cherished unkind feelings, if you have nourished envy and hatred, if you have cultivated in your hearts dislike and thoughts of vengeance, why then the more you are separated, the less you will be likely to carry out your unkind resolutions; and, in truth, if you have not cultivated kind feelings, gentle affections, regard, and love for one another, then all the other knowledge which you may have acquired may tend only to aggravate the spirit of unkindness, and to supply the weapons of ungenerous assault.

I speak plainly to you, my young friends, unless you make advances in the science of true affection, of regard for each other's rights, and especially for each other's feelings, (and you must learn to regard the feelings of your associates as a part of their rights not to be carelessly or unkindly invaded,) unless you have learnt these lessons, the others will at least be deprived of a large portion of their usefulness. Be gentle, be affectionate, one towards another, and let this not be a holiday virtue, but the continued study and progress of your life. It will give character and dignity to the acts of the future man; it will mould to the fulfilment of her heavenly mission the character of the woman. Yes, my young female friends, to you it is the life and the life's service of your sex. You must catch and practice every lesson of delicacy and affection which is imparted. You must strive to repress opposing feelings, and endeavor to give growth and exercise to all that is gentle in temper, and to all that is delicate in manner.

Ladies and Gentlemen, Teachers, I congratulate you upon the eminent success of your pupils. I know the responsibilities of your office, and how much of duty may be evaded without an evident violation of compact. You are conscientious, or these children could never have thus advanced. You must be conscientious, or they will never attain. What I have said to them of the necessity of study applies to you, my friends, as a duty of teaching. The moral must accompany the physical, and the heart must be dealt with as well as the head, and your children must learn from you the important lesson that they are to be social not selfish, and that it is more the consideration for others than for themselves that is to influence advantageously their future lives. The highest aim of a child should be to do right for the sake of that right, and to find a stimulent of effort in the good which that effort may achieve.

I see by these children's appearance, as I learn from their conduct, that they are beginning to understand the dignity of their character, and hence we may expect them to seek a course of conduct consistent with their estimate of themselves and their relatives. And your power of governing is to be in your influence over their affections and their attainments in self-knowledge. You have a right to their obedience, but you must acquire their love. We all know that circumstances may render physical discipline appropriate, but we all comprehend that the tone and language of affection draw back to virtue thousands who would have been hardened in vice by rigor.

The servant of the Prophet, you remember, when sent to raise the dead son of the Shunamitish woman, laid in vain the staff of his master upon the unconscious form of the child; but when the man of God himself went into the chamber and closed the door, and stretched himself upon the dead body with breast upon his breast and mouth to his mouth, then the genial warmth imparted gave back life to the little one, and restored joy and comfort to the household that was bereaved. So my friends—so you to whom are committed the character, the heart, and the life of this rising generation, send not the servant with the staff. When moral death seizes on the little one of your charge, send not the dependant with the rod, but go you into the chamber with him in secret where none but God can see, and there, hand to hand and breast to breast, warm the heart which error has chilled, and breathe anew into the dead moral form the breath of life and of love. Oh, give back to the heart-smitten parent the object of her prayers! Save, save the children of this Republic! Be you the benefactors of the Nation! Be you the servants of God!

Do not suppose, my friends, that one lesson, one monition is to fix a virtue or eradicate a fault—constancy of effort, unfailing example can alone profit. As well might the rose refer to a solitary sunbeam the beauty of its tint, or to a single zephyr the exquisitness of its order, as for a child to say what monition saved him from a practice of vice—what lesson of instruction fixed him in virtue.

It is a beautiful illustration of our institutions, and auspiciously ominous of their perpetuity, that the occasion is deemed of sufficient consequence to attract to the festival the honored Executive of the Nation.

Republicanism demands knowledge and virtue in the people, (the means of supplying that demand must be the proper object of solicitude with him to whom is entrusted the preservation of republican institutions,) and christianity in its great Author supplies the example of condescension to the wants, the manners, and the improvement of childhood ; and our children—these now around us—will feel their attachment to their country the stronger from the consciousness that every branch of that country's Government evinces an interest in their welfare.

Affection follows such a manifestation of interest, and the gratitude to the Chief Magistrate of the Nation for this day's kindness may ripen, in the bosom of these children, into the purest patriotism. Nothing binds man to his country more than a knowledge that his interest in the institutions is recognised ; and affection, respect, or gratitude for a Chief Executive Officer has often stood in place of love of country until it had come to be that which it supplied.

Gentlemen of the Board of Trustees, not the least gratifying portion of the exhibition which you this day make is the fact that your plan, thus extensively useful and capable of including every child in this District, is but of a few years trial, and the growth of the schools as rapid as the development of the scheme has been excellent. Every step of your progress is consequent upon previous success and increased confidence, and while it deserves the approval of every parent in the city, it commends itself to the favor and patronage of the National Legislature. You have established the means of general good in the centre of the Union. Let the representatives of every portion vie with each other in a liberal effort to sustain the institution that purifies the centre, and works thence in beneficial operation to the extremity. We ought not to doubt that a Legislature that has adopted this city, and shown its favor by liberal expenditures in the supply of physical conveniences and household comforts, will continue to manifest its maternal tenderness by generous appropriations to give character and usefulness to the generation that rises within its limits ; and this the more, as the benefits to flow from their kindness is not to be limited to the locality in which it originates, nor to operate in sectional divisions. The example will be beautifully effective throughout the Nation, and the influence upon the coming generation will be as diffusive as the excursive habits of our citizens. Near us is an institution which individual munificence endowed, and gifted and cultivated minds conduct for the promotion of the lofty branches of science and the arts. Let us all encourage in public schools the means of attaining the benefits of that endowment. Let us have no advantages of science, arts, or literature that shall not be accessble to all. Solitary knowledge gives pride to the possessor, and superstition to the uninformed. Diffused science is alone useful to the possessor and the public.

Gentlemen Trustees, the work in which you are engaged is one of patriotism and of philanthropy. The good you promote in behalf of these children—a part of our country—is reflected back upon yourselves, and will be blessed to your children. It is a stream of unfailing good. The ordinary work of benevolence perishes with its use: to-morrow, and to-morrow, and to-morrow, the supply must be renewed, or the beneficiary is lost. The supply which benevolence imparts in public schools has no decay, like the handful of meal in the barrel, and the oil in the widow's cruise, it knows no diminution. The benefits that so obviously flow from exertions to establish and maintain these schools, constantly provoke to additional exertions, while the necessity that demands it is so supplied that it may hereafter serve itself.

And since I have made the allusion to the meal-barrel and the oil-cruise, let me close my remarks by adding that the Prophet who blessed these vessels of the perishing widow and her son, derived his own nutriment from the benevolent office. May you, Gentlemen of the Board of Trustees. and you Ladies and Gentlemen Teachers, who do so much good to others, find in the heavenly office a support for your affection, and a reward for your benevolence; and, like the Prophet, may you sustain a life within by the outward demonstration of sympathy and beneficence.

HISTORICAL SKETCH

OF THE

PUBLIC SCHOOLS OF WASHINGTON.

The first election of the City Councils was held on the 17th June, 1802, and almost immediately after, notwithstanding the heavy expenses incurred in founding a new city in the wilderness, attention was given to the establishment of schools for the poor. The following is the preamble of a bill passed October 17th, 1805:

> "Impressed with a sense of the inseparable connexion between the education of youth and the prevalence of pure morals, with the duty of all communities to place within the reach of the poor as well as the rich the inestimable blessings of knowledge, and with the high necessity of establishing at the seat of the General Government proper seminaries of learning, the City Council do pass an act to establish and endow a permanent institution for the education of youth in the city of Washington."

By this act the sum of $1,500 was placed in the hands of a board of trustees, who were authorized to make adequate provision temporarily in private schools, at the expense of the city, for the education of children whose parents resided in the city and were unable to defray the expenses of their education. In 1808 the first school was established and placed under the care of a board of trustees, and provision was made for the reception of rather more than one hundred pupils, at at an expense of about $800. In 1816, an additional school was established. From 1820 to 1845, these two schools were conducted in part on the Lancasterian system, and the number of pupils averaged from two hundred and fifty to three hundred and fifty, annually. During most of the time but two teachers were employed, and the cost of the schools was about $1,700 a year. Occasional appropriations were, however, made in aid of charity schools under the care of benevolent individuals and churches. Into the two public schools none were admitted but such as were unable to pay for their tuition in private schools. Whenever pupils were found of peculiarly bright and active minds, the trustees were authorized to educate them in private schools of a higher grade, at the city expense. In 1826, the sum of $40,000 was appropriated, "and solemnly pledged and set apart forever," for the purpose of endowing public schools, and the Mayor was authorized to keep it vested in six per cent. stocks. This fund now, by careful management, amonnts to a little over $50,000.

In 1840 and 1841, the late Mayor, W. W. Seaton, Esq., (whose interest and zealous co-operation in the cause of public education should at all times be gratefully remembered and acknowledged,) called the attention of the Councils in vain to the expediency of extending the provisions for public school instruction. During the latter year, several individuals, who had investigated the subject, ascertained beyond a doubt, that out of a population of 5,200 children, between the ages of six and sixteen, not more than 1,200 were in the public and private schools of the city—a much smaller number was returned by the census. Thus it was evident that at least 4,000 children were growing up in ignorance, and the retributive effect of it was beginning to be viewed with alarm by reflecting citizens, in the character of the youthful population growing more and more immoral and vicious.

Serious and startling facts were placed in the possession of the Mayor, who, in his annual communication of 1842, earnestly invoked attention to the subject. The Mayor indicated that either the system then existing might be extended, or the New England system introduced; and any deficiency that might arise from the inadequacy of the income of the school fund could be provided for by a small tax on the assessed property of the city.

The Councils took up the subject, and in the lower board a committee, of which J. F. Halliday, Esq., now a trustee, and Rev. C. A. Davis were members, presented an able and eloquent report, understood to have been prepared by the efficient Secretary of the present board, accompanied by a bill for the establishment of seven public schools, open to all white children between six and sixteen years of age, to the number of about three thousand pupils. It also provided that they should be supported by a tax of one-sixth of one per cent., to be imposed upon the assessable property of the city.

So wide a departure from the system then existing, of educating only a portion of the indigent poor, to the one proposed of opening of the schools to all, to be enjoyed like the air we breathe, or the water we drink, or the streets through which we pass, could not but encounter serious opposition; and the idea of an additional tax was in the minds of many a fatal objection.

There was much earnest and excited discussion, and the attention of the people was more and more lead to the subject. The people met in their primary assemblies, and were addressed by gentlemen acquainted with the practical operations of the free-school system elsewhere, and communications constantly appeared in the *Intelligencer* and the *Sun*, whose columns were freely open to friends of reform. The subject was not allowed to rest. In the western part of the city the Union Fire Company freely and gratuitously threw open their comfortable and well-furnished hall, and for several winters had courses of lectures, and frequent meetings for the discussion of the free-school question. They were addressed by members of Congress and other gentlemen, the announcement of whose names would draw an audience; among others by Hon. J. Q. Adams, Mr. Justice Woodbury, Hon. Caleb Cushing, Hon. Charles Hudson, Rev. S. G. Bulfinch, Rev. E. E. Hale, and many others.

Such was the opposition that the free-school system encountered, the diversity of views respecting it, the doubts existing whether the city charter conferred sufficient power to impose taxes for the support of schools, and the expediency of imposing them, that the Mayor, in his annual communication of 1843, modified his views so far as to recommend simply the use of the entire interest of the school fund for school purposes, the establishment of an additional school, and the admission of pupils, other than the extremely poor, by the payment of a tuition fee of fifty cents monthly.

This combined free and pay system went into operation on the 1st of January, 1845, and continued till the 1st of September, 1848. Two new buildings were erected, at a cost of $6,300; four principal teachers and five assistants were employed, and accommodations were provided for seven hundred pupils. When the schools were first opened, and some time thereafter, they were nearly full, and the sum received from the pay pupils amounted to nearly enough ($1,050) to pay the assistants. But each year after the first, the total number of pupils diminished, as well as the receipts for tuition, till in 1848 the trustees reported to the councils that they had dismissed the assistant teachers in consequence of the tuition fees, to which they were restricted, being inadequate for their support. The average annual cost of the schools on this system was about $4,650. As the system which had been in operation till 1845 was defective, in educating only a portion of the youthful population, and at the same time fastening upon it the badge of poverty, and upon the schools the stigma of charity or pauper schools, so the system afterwards adopted was injudicious in bringing social distinctions into the school-room. The pupils soon ascertained which of their number were pay and which were free scholars, and it led to heart-burnings and ill-natured remarks among themselves and their respective parents. Injustice was often committed, through the natural pride of the extremely indigent, in preferring to pay the tuition fee (this tuition fee was fifty cents a month) rather than suffer the feelings of their children to be constantly wounded; while some in better circumstances avoided the payment if possible.

This state of things continued but a short time after the renewal of the charter by Congress, in which care was taken to obtain the power of imposing a school-tax, and also a capitation tax of one dollar annually on each voter, to be appropriated to the use of the public schools.

By several acts, passed since November 1, 1848, and the regulations of the board of trustees in accordance therewith, the schools of Washington are now conducted essentially on the same principles as those in the larger towns of Massachusetts. The schools are open freely to all white children, in the order of application, over the age of six years.

They are divided into primary and district schools, with a high school to go into operation in 1851.

There are fifteen primary schools taught by seventeen females and three males, and four district schools taught by four male principal teachers, and three female and two male assistants—in all twenty-nine teachers, to each of whom is assigned seventy pupils. In a portion of the primaries, females are only received; in others, males; and in the remainder, males and females. It has been found, wherever the sexes have been separated, that greater satisfaction has been given to the parents and teachers.

The studies in the *primary* schools are reading, writing, spelling, the powers of the letters, punctuation, mental and written arithmetic, geography, with landscape, linear and map-drawing, lessons on flowers, minerals, &c., vocal music, at the discretion of the teachers, with occasional lessons in plain sewing, fancy work, and embroidery.

To gain admittance to the *district* schools, the children must be found, by examination, capable of reading easy prose, of spelling correctly, well acquainted with the punctuation and abbreviation marks, with arithmetical figures and characters, notation, numeration, with the tables as far as ten of addition, subtraction, multiplication and division, and capable of performing simple operations in those rules.

The studies of the district schools include the above, with the powers of the letters, analysis and definitions of words, English grammar, with composition, elocution, book-keeping, history, arithmetic, and algebra, both mental and written, geometry, with its application to the measurement of surfaces and solids, philosophy, and physiology.

The expense of the present number of schools is about $12,000, of which $3,000 is derived from the interest of the school fund; about $5,000 from the capitation tax, and the remainder from the general fund of the city.

The system is highly popular, the schools are all full, and many applicants are on the list waiting for admission. The city having embarked in this enterprise, must continue to extend the system to meet the wants of the population. Additional primary schools are needed in all the districts of the city, as well as new and commodious buildings, furnished with comfortable seats and desks, and all the modern improvements, instead of some of the present ill-arranged, unventilated and inconvenient rooms now rented. A large expenditure will be needed to erect and put in operation the the high school which is authorized to be opened in 1851.

For all these objects, in view of what has already been accomplished, even with limited means, the popularity of the system with all classes, the perceptible improvement that has been effected in the character of the youthful population of the city by the public schools, and the importance of establishing, at the seat of the General Government, a system of public instruction, worthy of our institutions, and of the city that bears the name of Washington, that may be held up to all who assemble here from all parts of the country, and from foreign lands, with pride and satisfaction—the appeal is confidently made to the liberality of the Councils, and the Congress of the United States.

It will thus be seen that our schools are divided into primary districts, and a prospective high school. In the primary are received the young children, who here take their first lessons in learning. The modes of discipline and instruction provided for this class are widely different from those intended for the more advanced pupils. They cannot bear long confinement; their physical natures require frequent change. The eye, the ear, and the hand, are to be trained; objects must be presented for their examination, and much instruction given by conversation. The discipline of these tender and sensitive children must be mild, gentle, and parental. In the primary schools they are taught the elements of reading, writing, arithmetic, geography, grammar, vocal music, and drawing; and when thoroughly grounded in them, they are advanced into the district school. Here the discipline becomes more rigid, the course of study more extended, and the requirements greater.

The pupil is brought into severe and honorable competition with others, he learns properly to estimate his own powers, and in the contests of the school room prepare himself for the discipline of real life. If properly instructed at home and at the primary school, the pupil is prepared to enter the district school at the age of ten; after four or five years continuance here he may be presumed to be able to read and spell correctly, to have acquired a good knowledge of arithmetic, geography, and book-keeping, the history of his own country and some acquaintance with universal history, the Constitution of the United States and his duties as a citizen, some knowledge of the elements of geometry, at least so far as to enable him to take accurately the measurements of planes and solids; and, if he be industrious he will know something of physiology, surveying, and philosophy, together with the power of expressing simply and correctly his thoughts either orally or in writing.

The purpose of the district schools will not be accomplished unless they inspire every graduating pupil with a love of knowledge and with the determination by self-instruction to extend and perfect the education of which they lay the foundation.

Unless the pupil enters now upon his trade or selected vocation, he will pass into the high school where he will study more thoroughly several of the branches he had only commenced at the district school. He will enter upon an extensive mathematical course, extend his knowledge of physical science, perhaps apply himself to the ancient and modern languages, to intellectual and moral philosophy, and in a word, to those branches that will best fit him for the counting room, college, a trade, or professional life. Such briefly is the system, of which the foundation has here been laid, and which is in successful progress.

The importance of the classification of schools will be rightly understood by any one entering some private schools, where one or two teachers have their energies weakened, and their time frittered away in attempting to teach all things from the alphabet to the higher mathematics, together with three or four ancient and modern languages.

Again, its economy is a high recommendation of the public school system. In our public schools there are about 2,000 children. It is only reasonable to say, that in private schools the tuition of these children would be at least $10 each annually. In many of our private schools $50 or $60 is the usual price. But at the low rate mentioned, the cost would be $20,000, and double that sum would be a more correct estimate.

The expense of the existing public schools is nearly as follows:

Salaries of 4 Principals of District Schools	$2,800 00
Salaries of 5 Assistants in District Schools	1,250 00
Salaries of 15 Teachers of Primary Schools	3,750 00
Salaries of 5 Assistants in Primary Schools	1,000 00
Salary of Secretary of Board of Trustees	100 00
Contingent expenses of Board of Trustees	100 00
Rent of 13 rooms and lots	820 00
Fuel for schools	350 00
Contingent expenses of schools	1,830 00
Total	$12,000 00

It thus appears that the public schools may be well classified, and the instruction thorough and systematic; they can be conducted at a very moderate expense, and, at the same time, educate a large number of pupils.

There is barely room to hint at the strict responsibility to which the public schools are subjected, and the advantages resulting from educating, in a republican country, all classes together.

There are more pupils now in the private schools than there were in both the private and public five years since. There are more private schools and teachers than there were at that time. This is not so much due to the increase of our population as to the increased interest on the subject of education, and to the competition excited by the excellent manner in which the public schools have been conducted. Even if it were to happen that public schools should take the place of private ones, in a great measure, it would be for the advantage of the profession. The salaries of the teachers, of whom there would be a larger number than at present, would be greater and more regularly paid, they would be freed from many of the annoyances to which they are now subjected; nor would their real, (not nominal) compensation in most cases be much less than it now is.

In many instances, when Teachers of Private Schools have been candidates for situations in the Public Schools, they have always been elected in preference to others, where the qualifications were equal. The duty of recognizing the claims of those whose private establishments have been injured by the public schools has thus been acknowledged by the Board. At the last census only 986 pupils were returned as being in both the public and private schools of the city; there are now more than double that number in the public schools alone, and there are probably at least that number in the private schools, showing a largely increased per centage on the population of the city. The private schools are admitted on all hands, to be more numerous and more flourishing than at any time previously.

The friends of the private have no fears to apprehend from the rivalry of the public schools. Both are engaged in the same great and glorious object, the education of the rising generation, and working harmoniously together. At the late examinations many of the private teachers, both male and female, were present; and all unite most cordially, as members of the Columbian Association of Teachers, in promoting the important objects for which that Society was formed.

www.ingramcontent.com/pod-product-compliance
Lightning Source LLC
LaVergne TN
LVHW011144110826
845150LV00008B/2505

* 9 7 8 1 4 1 8 1 9 2 6 2 4 *